The Biernacki Geneaology

Margaret R. Biernaskie

Published by Margaret R. Biernaskie
4819 Round Lake Rd., Killaloe, Ontario K0J 2A0
Edited by Phyllis J. Biernaskie

Printed and bound by Doculink, Kanata, Ontario

ISBN 0-9736814-0-3

Table of Contents

Acknowledgments

We must keep our heritage alive from one generation to the next, so we do not forget where we came from. Through researching and recording the information in the form of a family tree, it will allow everyone for generations to come to reminisce and remember their heritage and roots.

I would like to acknowledge Shirley Mask Connolly a great deal of gratitude for her years of dedication to researching the polish records and providing the birth, death and marriage dates from Poland and the success in publishing her books, therefore keeping our Kashubian heritage alive. I would like to thank her for her guidance and permission to use quotes and pictures from her publishings.

Thank you to the many people who took the time to help me by allowing me to conduct interviews, for sharing pictures and stories and for the information on family ties: John Andrechek, Theresa Beanish, Raymond and Frances Biernaskie, Jack Biernacki, Leonard Buch, Elizabeth Byers (Beanish), Reverend Father Mervin Coulas, Clara Coulas (Blascavitch), Rita Coulas (Voldock), Evelyn Cybulskie (Vancuski), Reverend Father Norbert Cybulski, Laurie Dombroskie, Peter and Beverly Glofcheskie (Flynn), Barbara Goulet (Mintha), Agnes Herron (Biernaskie), Monica Kubisheskie (Vancuskie), Rita Maher, Rachel McGuey (Mask), Florence Peplinski (Biernaskie), Sylvester Peplinskie, Bernice Picotte, Catherine Prince (Blascavitch), Roger Prince, Theresa Prince (Kosnaskie), Donald Recoskie, Arthur Rumleskie and Noreen Vaillincourt (Andrechek).

Many thanks to Ron & Gerald Tracey on behalf of the Eganville Leader and Bonnie Summers, General Manager of the Barry's Bay This Week for the permission to use newspaper clippings and quotes from interesting articles, as well as Reverend Al Rekowski for excerpts taken from an article entitled "Breaking Out of The Wedge," printed in the This Week. Thanks also to Martha Prince at Doculink for her assistance in publishing this book. To my daughter Phyllis for editing this book and my husband Zigmund for his support and inspiration to achieve my goals. Please accept my apologies in advance for any errors or omissions. Once again many thanks.

Introduction

This book is lovingly dedicated to the Antoine and Brigid Biernacki (nee Lilla) ancestors who were one of the first settlers to land in Canada and settle in Sherwood Township in the County of Renfrew.

Excerpt taken from Shirley Mask Connolly: Antoine Biernacki originated in the parish of Parchowo, West Prussia, who may have married Regina Charlotte Neuman (nee Grunow), a widow four or five years older than Antoine. He married Brigid Lilla on November 20, 1855 in Parchowo, Poland and they had three children, which were born in West Prussia. On July 16, 1868, they arrived in Canada from Hamburg, Germany on the ship Franz De Paul Armesan. They appeared on the 1871 census of Madawaska East and on January 23, 1873, they officially located on Lot 31, Concession 6 of Sherwood Township. Antoine Biernacki swore an affidavit stating that he had resided on the Sherwood Township property for four years (circa 1868-1869) or probably since he arrived in Canada. By January 1873, he indicated that they had ten acres of land cleared and cultivated and a house, barn and stable on the property. The house was 18x19 feet and the barn was 18x30 feet.

Guide to Reading Family History Charts

The children of Antoine and Brigid Biernacki are organized into individual sections. Each descendant is placed oldest to youngest. Each section has a chart devoted to the parents and lists each dependant. Then the dependant is categorized based on birth dates with roman numerals in rows. When each dependant of the family is listed, their dependants are also listed in numerical order.

Historic polish surnames are gender specific. Male surnames end with an "i" ex. John Biernacki and female surnames end with an "a" ex. Martha Biernacka. The future generations have now made slight changes to the spelling of their surnames. Every effort has been made to include all names of spouses and birth and death dates.

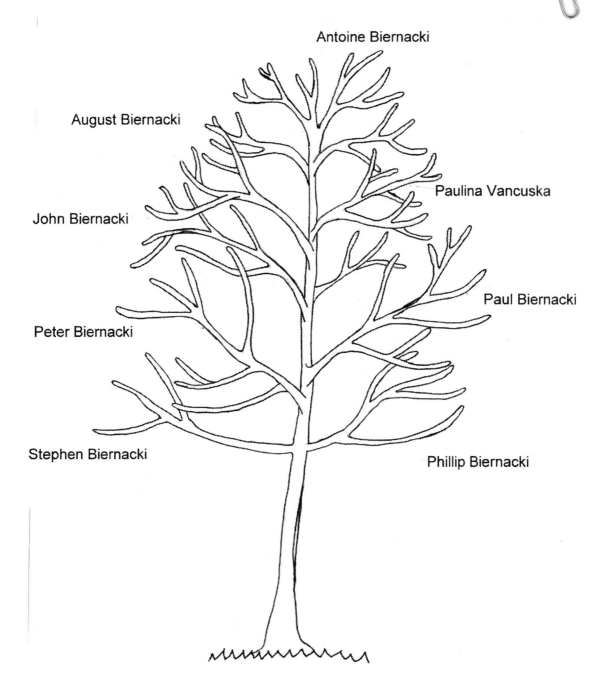

Antoine Biernacki

August Biernacki

Paulina Vancuska

John Biernacki

Peter Biernacki

Paul Biernacki

Stephen Biernacki

Phillip Biernacki

BIERNACKI FAMILY TREE

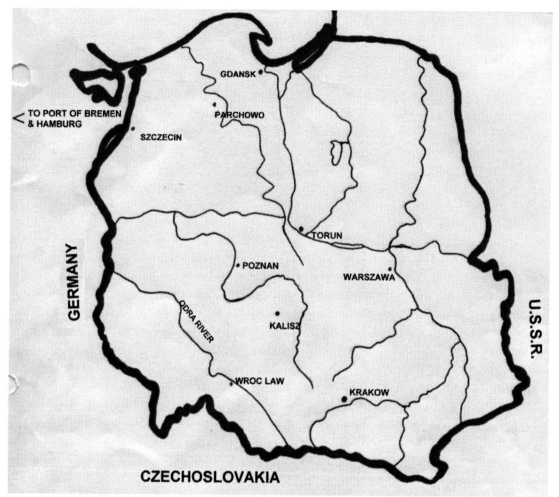

MAP OF POLAND

Excerpts taken from "Breaking Out of the Wedge," written by " Reverend Al Rekowski and printed in the Barry's Bay This Week, quotes:

> *From Radecki-Heydenkorn in: A member of a distinguished family: The Polish group in Canada- 1976 states unequivocally: "The First Kashubs arrived in Quebec in 1858 from the German Port of Bremen. Since they continued to come in small groups from 1858-1895, no doubt different groups embarked on ships sailing out of either port, since the two ports were not that far from each other; the evidence seems to point to Hamburg as the port of embarkation for most groups. The parents of Monsignor Biernacki spoke of Hamburg as the port where their parents started their ocean voyage."*

Leaving their homeland of Parchowo, West Prussia, they reached Szczecin on the Odra River and crossed into the Port of Hamburg, Germany. There they embarked their ship, the Franz de Paul Armesan and set sail for Canada.

THE FAMILY

OF

ANTOINE & BRIGID NEE (LILLA)

BIERNACKI

Family Tree of ANTOINE & BRIGID (LILLA) BIERNACKI

NAME	BORN	DIED	SPOUSE	BORN	DIED	MARRIAGE etc.
I. Antoine Biernacki	West Prussia 1801	Wilno Nov 5, 1884	Brigid Lilla	Poland 1835	Siberia Mar 20,1920	Parchowo Poland Nov 20,1855
Children:						
1.August Biernacki	Prussia Aug 9,1856	Aug 26,1936	Marianna Peplinska	Prussia 1869	Oct 22,1942	July 13,1884
2. Paulina Vancuska	Parchowo June 4,1859	Sept 13,1939	Adam Vancuski		Feb 27,1921	Brudnell Feb 8,1875
3. John Biernacki	Oct 23, 1863	June 13, 1949	Augustina Retza	June 16, 1872		Wilno Nov 4,1890
4. Paul Biernacki	Feb 7, 1869	May 27, 1942	1.Marianna Yakubuska 2.Marianna Rekowska			Apr 30, 1884 Jan 25, 1902
5. Peter Biernacki	Aug 31, 1872	Nov 21, 1913 Whitney	Anna Lukaszewitz		Oct 22, 1960	Wilno Mar 7, 1905
6. Phillip Biernacki	1876	May 25, 1935				Drowned at Fort Frances, Ontario
7. Stephen Biernacki						No Records

August and Marianna Biernacki
Collection of the late Theresa Beanish

August Biernacki and Marianna Peplinska with their children Evelyn, Martha and
Beatrice at the Biernaski's Golden Wedding Anniversary in 1935
Collection of the late Theresa Beanish

The Biernacki homestead where the early pioneers settled. Zigmund Biernaski is seen here with his father John and horses Charlie and Jesse with Dog Whiskey. Photo taken in 1959. *Collection of Dolores Flynn*

Biernacki family members- back row: Martha BIERNACKA, Mary Anne MASK, John BIERNACKI, Beatrice BIERNACKA, August BIERNASKI and Agatha BIERNACKA. Front row: Evelyn OGILVIE (Mask) and Evelyn Olson. *Collection of Zigmund Biernaski*

St. Hedwig's Church, 1920
Collection of Arthur Rumleskie, clipping from the Eganville Leader

B. Row L. to R.: John Biernacki, Paul Mask
M. Row L. to R.: Unknown, children unknown, Anastasia Jercha with
            Doris Mae, Mariana Mask, Annie Andrechek
F. Row L. to R.: Beatrice, Martha, Marianna, August Biernacki and
            Evelyn Olson
Collection of Zigmund Biernaski

THE FAMILY

OF

AUGUST & MARIANNA NEE

(PEPLINSKA)

BIERNACKI

Family Tree of AUGUST & MARIANNA (PEPLINSKA) BIERNACKI

NAME	BORN	DIED	SPOUSE	BORN	DIED	MARRIAGE etc.
I. August Biernacki	Prussia Aug 9, 1856	Aug 26, 1936	Marianna Peplinska	Prussia 1869	Oct 22, 1942	July 13, 1884
Children:						
1. John A. Biernacki	June 24, 1885	Jan 30, 1973	Johanna Coulas Agatha Maika (Kosnacka)	Jan 6, 1900 Jan 6, 1894	Sept 6, 1953 May 5, 1972	June 1921 Aug 20, 1958
2. Annie Andrecheck	Sept 9, 1886	June 12, 1975	John Andrecheck	Mar 27, 1883	Dec 31, 1953	June 19, 1910
3. Rev. Msgr. Peter B. Biernacki	May 18, 1888	Dec 31, 1958				Ordained into priesthood Dec 21, 1910
4. Maryann Mask	Jan 1, 1890	May 3, 1979	Paul B. Mask	Feb 14, 1885	Nov 13, 1964	June 24, 1913
5. Anastasia Jercha	Dec 1, 1891	Dec 19, 1952	Ignatius J. Jercha	Jarochin, Poznan July 19, 1893	Hammond, Indiana U.S.A. Nov 17, 1971	Barry's Bay
6. Anthony Biernacki	Jan 2, 1895	June 2, 1971	Clara Hildebrandt	1905	Apr. 14, 1979	July 1926
7. Martha Biernacka	Oct 15, 1896	June 2, 1986				
8. Bronas Biernacki	Sept 15, 1900	Nov 10, 1975				Served in the Canadian Forces 1939- 1945
9. Beatrice Biernacka	Feb 24, 1902	Feb 17, 1982				
10. Evelyn Olson	Dec 6, 1904		Otto Olson			

Msgr. Biernacki

Collection of Roseann Shalla

In Memory of
Rt. Reverend Monsignor
Peter B. Biernacki
Parish Priest of St. Hedwig's,
Barry's Bay
BORN MAY 18th, 1888
ORDAINED DECEMBER 21st, 1910
DIED DECEMBER 31st, 1958

R. I. P.

Collection of Zigmund Biernaski

Msgr. Biernacki and his car at Alexander Shalla and Elizabeth
Etmanskie's wedding August 10, 1915. *Collection of Peter Glofcheskie*

Monsignor Peter B. Biernacki

August and Marianne Biernacki (nee Peplinska), born in West Prussia, came to Canada to start a new life with their children. Born and raised as Roman Catholic Kashubians, they brought with them their culture, language and heritage; their way of life left behind. They settled on Lot 31 Concession 6 of Sherwood Township. They continued farming, raising a family of ten children, in which their siblings worked with them, and others who were fortunate to leave home and were successful in pursuing an education in order to serve people in need. Besides farming, August was an attendance officer at St. Josephs High School.

Barry's Bay was home to a prominent citizen, a leader in the 1900's, one who fostered the idea of building a hospital: Monsignor Peter B. Biernacki. Growing up as a young boy, he focused his talents as an athlete, which inspired him to pursue other interests and dreams later in life. As a man of great stature and strong leadership, he dedicated his vocation to serve his people as a spiritual leader. With the support of the community and beyond, his vision of the future was strong and hopeful.

Peter was born May 8, 1888, the son of August and Marianne Biernacki (nee Peplinska), was one of a family of ten children, who grew up in the Barry's Bay area. As a young boy he was educated here, where he completed grade eight at Wilno Separate School. With Baseball being his main hobby, he had a chance to play a sport he loved. Some teammates included Henry Chapeskie, Jack Cyra, John and Peter Drohan, Tom, Charlie, William, Mick and Dan Murray. Having perfected this sport over a number of years, he was offered the chance to play professionally in Detroit, Michigan. However, his strong will for his faith and love of his people directed him to enter into the priesthood to serve god. Therefore, he turned down the opportunity as a professional baseball player. He attended the Polish Seminary at Orchard Lake in Michigan, where he completed high school, college and theology. He was the First Canadian born of polish extraction to be ordained into the priesthood on December 21, 1910 at the age of twenty-two in Wilno by his lordship Bishop Scollard of North Bay, Ontario. Under the direction of Father Jankowski, he served as an assistant priest in Wilno as well as he served the congregation at Our Lady of Assumption in Barry's Bay twice a month.

Father Jankowski saw a great need for a church to be built in Barry's Bay due to the influx of polish immigrants to the area. Father Biernacki was then appointed to construct St. Hedwig's Church. Volunteers from the catholic community and trades people gathered to build St. Hedwig's in 1914. The first mass; midnight mass was celebrated on Christmas Eve by Father Biernacki. Bishop Ryan blessed the church in 1915 and the bell was named Bronislaus, Peter, Stanislaus, and Hedwig. Father Biernacki along with the help of fellow parishioners organized the outdoor church picnics, which there were lots of fun and games. This event was held annually during the summer for many consecutive years to help raise funds for the financial needs of the church. He had a strong will and determination to achieve what he did and from there he worked tirelessly to meet the needs of the people of his parish and the community as a whole in the Madawaska Valley.

A large rectory was established in 1922 to accommodate the visiting bishops and fellow priests on special events. A convent for the sisters of St. Joseph's was also established by Father Biernacki in 1928, as well as a St. Joseph's Separate School in 1930. He and Henry Chapeskie met with Bishop Ryan in Pembroke to obtain a lease to build St. Joseph's on church property. The convent was home to the sisters of St. Joseph where they taught in an eight room school house.

On the 25th anniversary of his ordination, Father Biernacki was given the title of domestic prilate, Rt. Reverend Monsignor. He was a spiritual leader in St. Hedwig's parish for forty-four years. Aside from his pastoral duties; Monsignor Biernacki took time out for his leisure activities. He had continued to play the game of baseball with his comrades and often visited his childhood homestead for family gatherings. By integrating well with the people in the entire community he gained much respect, trust and friendship. He had the opportunity to own his first 1915 Model A car, which was a privilege and tradition for the parish priest to make his annual visitations to every household of the parish. On one occasion Monsignor Biernacki and his brother John traveled to various parts of the United States and to visit their sisters in Hammond, Indiana.

Monsignor Biernacki owned a movie projector and camera, in which he took many silent movies of special family gatherings and events such as hunting and fishing. Also in the years of 1949-1953, he showed family movies in the church basement on Friday and Sunday nights at 8:00pm to raise funds for the parish and the building of the hospital. Norbert Cybulskie in his youth had the privilege to operate the movie projector for Monsignor. His responsibility as well was to pick up these 16 mm sound production tapes at the train station, where they were shipped from Ottawa by train. Norbert Cybulskie was educated at St. Joseph's Separate School in Barry's Bay and completed grade thirteen at St. Andrew's Separate School in Killaloe. From there he attended the Polish Seminary at Orchard Lake, Michigan, where he completed his theology at St. Paul's Seminary in Ottawa. Reverend Father Norbert Cybulskie was ordained into priesthood on June 3, 1962, at St. Hedwig's Church and celebrated his first mass on June 10, 1962.

Leisure times were also spent at his summer cottage on Ski Island located on Lake Kaminiskeg and Hydes Bay on the Madawaska River. His favorite trips were made to Opeongo River, five miles from Victoria Lake as well as Tea Lake in Quebec, where he and his friends hunted deer and moose.

His last vision was to build a hospital, which was in dire need to serve the surrounding community of Barry's Bay for many miles. He worked diligently and in 1948 he was instrumental for his dream to become a reality; he never did get to see the fruits of his labor. His ailing health forced him to hand the reigns of this project to Henry Chapeskie to complete. Monsignor Peter B. Biernacki passed away on December 31, 1958 at the age of seventy.

It was Monsignor Biernacki's vision and efforts that contributed greatly to the Barry's Bay Community through the resurrection of a church, rectory, separate school, convent and a vision of a hospital. Since that time, changes have evolved, but the true remains of his work are still evident and continue to grow with prosperity of new visions.

Pic of the Past

Teresa Beanish lent Barry's Bay This Week this photo
of her uncle, Monsignor Biernaskie, receiving the Polish
Medal from Henry Chapeski. Both were involved in de-
veloping the Village of Barry's Bay. This photo was tak-
en in late November 1958, less than two weeks before
Msgr. Biernaskie's death.   photo/MONTAIGNE

Collection of Elizabeth Byers (of the Barry's Bay This Week)

Msgr. Biernacki at his cottage at Hydes Bay, Comberemere.
Collection of Dolores Flynn (niece)

Msgr. Biernacki and Fr. Paul Jolkowski in Round Lake
Collection of Dolores Flynn

St. Hedwig's Cemetery Barry's Bay, On
Collection of Beverly Glofcheskie

Our choice from the archives this week is the record of two of Barry's Bay's baseball stars. According to the donor of our photograph the player pictured on the right is the Great Biernaskie, the man who put Barry's Bay on the map with his baseball fame. The man on the left is Thomas Patrick Murray, Biernaskie's catcher for a three year stint of baseball play in the Bay. Murray was the catcher for the Barry's Bay team for 30 years. The picture was taken in 1910 in the Township of Jones. Biernaskie went on to be educated at St. Mary's College in Detroit Michigan and was ordained to the priesthood in 1910. As a reminder to Bancroft and North Hastings residents the "Pic of the Past" series will continue in the new weekly publication for your area, **the bancroft-north hastings weekly.** Readers who have memory-lane photographs they would like printed may send them to the **weekly, Box 1120, Bancroft, Ontario.**

Collection of Bancroft-North Hastings Weekly

Msgr. Biernacki and comrades who gathered for a banquet at his cottage at Hydes Bay in Combermere. Left to right are: Fr. Ambrose Pick, Charles Murray, Tom Murray, Msgr. Biernacki, Fr. Ritza, Fr. McNamara, Bernard Murray and Anthony Biernacki. *Collection of Dolores Flynn (niece)*

Left to right - Horace Landon, Peter H. Etmanski, Father Biernacki, Anthony Prince, Thomas Conway Sr., Bishop Ryan (seated) at official opening of St. Joseph's School in May 1930.

Collection unknown

The Three Biernacka Nurses

Three daughters of August and Marianne; Martha, Beatrice and Evelyn Biernacka left their native home in Barry's Bay and moved to Hammond, Indiana U.S.A. to pursue careers in nursing. They were the first girls to become registered nurses from Barry's Bay. Martha graduated from St. Margaret's School of Nursing in Hammond, Indiana. She was a clinical instructor and ward supervisor for over fifty-five years at St. Margaret's Hospital. She was also a member of Indiana State Nurse's Association of St. Margaret's Alumni; as well as a member of St. Andrew's Church of Calumet City, Indiana.

Beatrice received her formal training at St. Joseph's Hospital nursing school in Sudbury, Ontario. She was an obstetrical supervisor for many years and an anesthetist at St. Margaret's Hospital in Hammond, Indiana. She was also a member of Indiana State Nurses Association and a member of St. Andrew's Church, Calumet City, Indiana. Indiana was home for Martha and Beatrice during their days of youth as well as their retirement, but their wishes were to be interred at St. Hedwig's Cemetery in Barry's Bay, Ontario at their time of passing.

Evelyn Olsen (nee Biernacka) worked for five years as a sales lady with J.R. Hazelton in Killaloe, Ontario, when she too left Barry's Bay and moved to Hammond, Indiana U.S.A. to become a nurse in training at St. Margaret's Hospital. She graduated as a nurse as well and it was there she met and married Otto Olson and they raised two children: Jerry and Phyllis Rae.

Anastasia Biernacka

Anastasia Biernacka married Ignatius Jercha in Barry's Bay and took up residence in North Cobalt. To their misfortune their residence was burned down in a forest fire in 1922. They then moved to Hammond, Indiana U.S.A. To this union were born two children: Doris Mae who married Ted Jamka and son Julien Jercha. It was Julien, a nephew of Msgr. Peter B. Biernacki; who followed his footsteps and graduated from the University Of Orchard Lake, Michigan, U.S.A. and was ordained into the priesthood at Sacred Heart Church, Notre Dame University in South Bend, Indiana on June 7, 1950. Farther Jercha was a frequent visitor to Barry's Bay over the years, keeping in touch with his many relatives and friends in the area. He was a spiritual director and pastor of St. Anthony's Parish, Fish Lake Walkerton, Indiana. He passed away on June 27, 1987.

THE THREE
EVELYN ARE

Pic of the past

Biernacki sisters, Martha, Beatrice and
the daughters of the late Mr. and Mrs.
nacki of Barry's Bay. They were the
AUGUST

first registered nurses from Barry's Bay. This
picture was taken in 1925.

Collection of Barry's Bay This Week

Beatrice and Martha Biernacka taken at Barry's Bay at brother John Biernacki's
funeral in 1973.
Collection of Zigmund Biernaski

Evelyn Olson with nephews August and Zigmund Biernaski at the original homestead
where Evelyn was born. *Collection of Zigmund Biernaski*

Evelyn and Otto Olson with daughter Phyllis Rae on Christmas Day in the U.S.A.
Collection of Dolores Flynn

Evelyn and Otto Olson with children Phyllis Rae and Jerry in Phoenix, Arizona.
Collection of Zigmund Biernaski

Mary Anne Biernacka

Mary Anne Biernacka married Paul B. Mask on June 24, 1913 in Barry's Bay. In the days of her youth, she taught school in Paugh Lake, Barry's Bay and Round Lake. They took up residence on an island in Barry's Bay below St. Hedwig's Church known today as "Mask Island" in March of 1918 and it was there they farmed their entire life as well as operated a dairy in the village. They were blessed with nine children and everyone had the task of helping out with chores. At present day the farm is still being farmed and continues to be operated by the Mask family, a grandson; Raymond JR.

Theresa Beanish (nee Mask)

Theresa Mask, a daughter of Mary Anne and Paul Mask married Adam Beanish on June 24, 1947 and they raised five children. Theresa was very much involved in volunteer work throughout her life. Theresa and her mother Mary Anne started a fundraising campaign for the building of a hospital being Msgr Peter B. Biernacki as the founder. After the hospital was built they founded the St. Francis Memorial Hospital Auxiliary with other women. She continued her volunteer work at the hospital all her life for the auxiliary of the Royal Canadian Legion, Barry's Bay branch and the Sacred Heart League at St. Hedwig's Catholic Church. She received many honors for her work and her wonderful personality went far and wide. She was surrounded by many friends; lending a helping hand in anyone's need, whether it was visiting relatives or friends to attending weddings, praying the rosary at wakes or her story telling and jokes of great laughter. She passed away December 19, 2002 at the age of 85 years at St. Francis Memorial Hospital.

Bronas Biernacki

Excerpts taken from "Barry's Bay This Week": Bronas Biernacki was born in Barry's Bay, Ontario and in his early years, he worked for the Bank of Montreal and later transferred to Western Canada, where he worked for the Bank of Montreal in Yorkton, Regina Saskatchewan and Winnipeg, Manitoba. During World War II, he served in the armed forces overseas from 1939-1945. After the war, he returned to Winnipeg, where he worked in the real estate business. He passed away at the age of 75 and was interred in the brookside cemetery in Winnipeg, Manitoba.

Paul and Mary-Ann Mask (nee Biernacka) married June 24, 1913. *Collection Elizabeth Byers (granddaughter)*

Picture of Rev. Father Julien Jercha from Walkerton, Indiana visiting relatives in Barry's Bay. Left to right are Zigmund Biernaski, Martha Biernacka, Theresa Beanish (nee Mask), Father Julien and in front Barry Biernaskie. *Collection of Zigmund Biernaski*

Adam and Theresa Beanish (nee Mask) on their wedding day.
Collection of Elizabeth Byers

The 50th wedding anniversary of MaryAnn and Paul Mask was celebrated on June 24, 1963. All family members include left to right are: Sylvia Lamont, Clementine Larson, Leona Drury, Theresa Beanish, Florence Kosnaskie, Evelyn Ogilvie, Mary Ann, Paul Mask, Donald, Elmer and Raymond Sr. Mask. *Submitted to the This Week from Elizabeth Byers*

Father Julien Jercha, son of Anastasia and Ignatius Jercha.
Collection from This Week Newspaper

Theresa Beanish was presented a Millennium plaque by Renfrew County Council recently. Mrs. Beanish has been an active volunteer at the Valley Manor Nursing Home, St. Francis Memorial Hospital, The Opeongo Seniors and at church and community functions for at least the past 40 years. Picture was taken on Jan 31, 2001 in Pembroke.
Photo of This Week from Elizabeth Byers

Beverly Glofcheski, daughter of Patrick Sr. and Dolores Flynn (nee Biernaski) and Donald Kosnaskie, son of James and Florence Kosnaskie (Mask). Taken at the Wilno Heritage celebrations in 2003. *Collection of Beverly Glofcheski*

Anthony & John Biernacki's Sawmill

Anthony Biernacki married Clara (nee Hildebrandt) on July 1926 and raised four children. They resided in Barry's Bay, where Tony and his brother John operated the remains of the sawmill. Their father August bought the mill from Fred Armstrong; shingle mill and a small three sided planning mill. Later the two brothers parted and Anthony went to work in the local sawmill as a third class stationary engineer, as well as the Chapeskie lumber company at Barry's Bay and the Drohan lumber company at McPhees Bay. He also worked as an engineer with Murray Bros. steam powered sawmill at Madawaska until the sawmill was destroyed by fire on November 13, 1970.

John and Johanna (nee Coulas) Biernacki were married in June of 1921 and took up residence on the homestead of his father August Biernacki, and to this union was born two sons, August and Zigmund. John and his brother Anthony operated the remains of the saw mill, their father August bought from Fred Armstrong, a shingle mill, and a small three sided planning mill. Later the two brothers parted and John tilled the land on his farm to make a living, besides cutting timber on his wood lot during the winter months. He operated his own saw mill, shingle, and grist mill on the farm, powered by a steam engine he owned. It was a 1923 portable steam engine and is now owned and rebuilt by Wayne Houston from the Western Part of Ontario and can be seen in various shows and fairs.

A 1923 Portable steam engine owned and operated by John A. Biernacki in the 1950's and now rebuilt and owned by Wayne Houston. *Collection of Zigmund Biernaski*

St. Hedwig's church in the early 1920's, Murray and Omarnique saw mills in the far background. Nearest to the church is Anthony and John Biernacki's saw mill, planer and shingle mills. Pervious owner was Fred Armstrong. *Collection of Arthur Rumleskie and Eganville Leader*

Picture of the Fred Armstrong mill owed in 1914 and later owned and operated by the Biernacki family. *Collection of Arthur Rumleskie and Eganville Leader*

Anthony and Claire Biernacki and sister Beatrice Biernacka kneeling, in
1925. *Collection of Dolores Flynn*

Anthony Biernacki and son Stanley celebrating his First Confirmation.
Collection of Dolores Flynn

Stanley and Dolores Biernaski, children of Anthony and Clara Biernacki.
Collection of Dolores Flynn

Jack Andrecheck and Annie Biernacka's wedding photo June, 1910.
Collection of Shirley Mask Connolly

Photo at left is John Biernacki and sister Beatrice at their young age and at right is Anthony and Clara Biernacki with Jude on the left and the child on the right is unknown. *Collection of Zigmund Biernaski*

John Biernacki and Ambrose Dombroskie, owner of threshing mill after a day of threshing on John A. Biernacki's farm. *Collection of Dolores Flynn*

Picture of John and Johanna Biernacki. Left to right are: Zigmund, John, Johanna (nee Coulas) and August. *Collection of Zigmund Biernaski*

Biernacki Homestead Barry's Bay, On
Collection of Zigmund Biernaski

A pine china cupboard from the John Biernacki homestead and may have been owned by his ancestors. Now owned by an individual. *Collection of Zigmund Biernaski*

Zigmund and Margaret Biernaskie and Family
Mike Weisand Photography

Msgr. Biernacki's summer cottage on Ski Island in Barry's Bay.
Collection of Shirley Mask Connolly

Family Tree of AUGUST BIERNACKI

John A. Biernacki

NAME	DIED	SPOUSE	DIED	MARRIAGE etc.
I. August Biernaski	June 14, 1993	Diane Woodbridge		Oct. 1966
Children:				
1. Rodney Biernaskie		Natalie Barrington		May 8, 2004
II. Zigmund Biernaski		Margaret Dombroskie		July 2, 1966
Children:				
1. Barry Biernaskie		Colleen Stewart		Sept. 26, 1998
2. Phyllis Biernaskie				

Annie Andrecheck

NAME	DIED	SPOUSE	DIED	MARRIAGE etc.
I. Edmund Andrecheck	Sept. 5, 1993	1.Martha Vachon 2. Agnes Kelly	May 1964	
Children:				
1. Beverly Bentley		John Bentley		
Ch: Christina				
Eric				
Craig				
Adam				
Jessica				
2. Marie Denbow		Dennis Denbow		
Ch: Simone				
Cabot				
3. Joan Berubeau		Lucien Berubeau		
Ch: Andre James				
Noel				
4. Martha Gray		John Gray		
Ch: Heather				
Sarah				
5. Peter Andrecheck		Linda Howard		
Ch: Blair				
Erin				
II. Martha Cybulski		Harold Cybulski	May 12, 1991	
Children:				
1. Sylvia Kennedy		George Kennedy		
Ch: Marty				
Brian				
Cregg				
Daryl				

2. Mary Jane Hardy Ch: Roger Hardy Michaela 3.Susan Hudder Ch: Jeffery Melodie		1.Roger Hardy 2.Murray McBride Richard Hudder		
III. Agnes Coulas Children: 1. Brian Coulas Ch: Meredith Brent 2. Daniel Coulas 3. Jerome Coulas Ch: Marla Benjamin 4. Peter Coulas 5. Paul Coulas	Dec.30, 1988	Lawrence Coulas Mary Ellen Barbara Joan Sally Donna	May 29, 1986	
IV. Raymond Andrecheck	Feb.14, 1975	Ann McCann		No Children
V. Lawrence Andrecheck Children: 1. Noreen Vaillincourt Ch: Jason Curtis 2. Stella Andrecheck 3. Kevin Andrecheck 4. Ruth Andrecheck	Apr. 7, 1970	Irene O'Hara James Vaillincourt	Mar. 22, 1984	
VI. AnnMae Warren Children: 1. Patricia Warren 2. Louise Warren 3. Joan Warren		William Warren		
VII. Bronas Andrecheck Children: 1. Michael Andrecheck Ch: Michelle Philippe 2. John Andrecheck 3. Janet Wilson Ch: Melanie Ben 4. Sharon Hops Ch: Adam Brandon		Josephine Maika Nicole Brunet Donna Anderson Tok Wilson Steve Hops		

Rev. MSGR. Peter B. Biernacki

NAME	DIED	SPOUSE	DIED	MARRIAGE etc.
Rev. Msgr. Peter B. Biernacki	Dec. 31, 1958			Ordained into priesthood Dec. 21, 1910

Mary Ann Mask

NAME	DIED	SPOUSE	DIED	MARRIAGE etc.
I. Evelyn Ogilvie	Aug. 26, 1991	John Ogilvie	Apr.23, 1974	No children

II. Florence Kosnaskie
 	
Children:
    1. Jerry Kosnaskie
    2. Donald Kosnaskie
    Ch: Shane
    Jamie
	Dec. 6, 1968	1. James Kosnaskie
		
		2. John Shalla
			Oct. 29, 1954
			Dec. 9, 1997
			
			Jan 2005	

III. Teresa Beanish
 	
Children:
    1. Phyllis Rae Leveque
    Ch: Kathleen
        Dennis
    2.Louise Mae Beanish
    3. Ann Marie Leveque
    Ch: Peter
        Michelle
    4. Elizabeth Byers
    Ch: Lawrence
        Paul
        Ellen
    5. Gerard Paul Beanish
    Ch: Adam
        Jessica
	Dec 19, 2002	Adam Beanish
		
		Lawrence Leveque
		
		Michael Leveque
		
		Lawrence Byers
		
		Janet Hitchinson
			Sept 13, 1979	Sept. 18, 1976

IV. Raymond Mask
 	
Children:
    1. Susan Sech
    Ch: Tyler
        Andrew
        Shelly
    2. Bonnie Mask
    3. Patricia Brown
    Ch: Marilyn
        Mathew
	June 27, 1998	Marilyn Bonnie
		
		Steve Sech
		
		David Brown
			Sept. 21, 1995	

Jonathon
4. James Mask
Ch: Kimberly
    Cassandra
5. Rachel McGuey
Ch: Christina
    Melissa
    Candace
6. Peter Mask
Ch: Safron
    Sloan
7. Raymond Mask Jr.
Ch: Derek
    Scott
8. Paul Mask
Ch: Allison
9. Michael Mask
Ch: Brock
    Bryden
		Robert McGuey
		
		Shelly Scott
		
		Becky Maika
				Oct. 8, 1983

V. Leona Drury
Children:
  1. Wayne Drury
  2. Betty Craig
  3. Bonnie Valerie
		Len Drury
		
		Emily McEwen
		Brian Craig
		Max Valerie
			Dec.1995	

VI. Clementine Larson Children: 1. Eric Larson		John Larson		
VII. Elmer Mask Children: 1. Christopher Mask	Feb. 10, 1986	1. Virginia Wheeler 2. Lena Mascovitch	1962	
VIII. Sylvia Lamont		James Lamont		

IX. Donald Mask
Children:
  1. Ingrid Hassani
  Ch: Bechir
    Rasael
  2. Adrian Mask
  Ch: Eve
		Eva Pilar
		
		Lotsi Hassani
		
		Julie		

Anastasia Jercha

NAME	DIED	SPOUSE	DIED	MARRIAGE etc.
I. Rev. Father Julien Jercha	June 27, 1987			Ordained into priesthood on June 7, 1950
II. Doris Mae Jamka Children: 1. Michael Jamka 2. Kenny Jamka 3. Christine Jamka		1. Ted Jamka 2. Frank Palikan		

Anthony Biernacki

NAME	DIED	SPOUSE	DIED	MARRIAGE etc.
I. Stanley Biernaskie Children: 1. Jack Biernaskie 2. Keith Biernaskie 3. Marilyn Biernaskie 4. Sheraly Biernaskie 5. James Biernaskie	Apr. 5, 1980	Marilyn Redford		
II. Mary Biernaskie	1930			Died in infancy
III. Doloris Flynn Children; 1.Beverly Glofcheskie Ch: Sarah Samuel Natalie 2. Patrick Jr. Flynn Ch: Dawn Patrick Erin	Jan. 10, 1999	Patrick J. Flynn Peter Glofcheskie Lorraine May	Dec. 11, 2002	Sept. 16, 1952
IV. Jude Biernaski	Jan. 28, 1996			

Martha Biernacka

Martha pursued a career in nursing and moved to the United States. She never married.

Bronas Biernacki

Bronas served in the Canadian Armed Forces from 1939- 1945 and never married. He lived in Winnipeg, Manitoba and was buried there.

Beatrice Biernacka

Beatrice pursued a career in nursing in the United States and never married.

Evelyn Olson

NAME	DIED	SPOUSE	DIED	MARRIAGE etc.
I. Gerald Olson Children: 1. Charles Lee Olson 2. Mary Ellen Olson		1. Mary Ellen Musselman 2. Hariet Graves		1962
II. Phyllis Rae Musselman Children: 1. John Mussleman 2. Daniel Musselman 3. Julianna Rae Saiz 4. ChristinaMusselman 5. Rebecca Musselman 6. Peter Musselman		John Musselman Jonathan Saiz		 July 25, 1992

THE FAMILY

OF

PAULINA & ADAM

VANCUSKI

Family Tree of PAULINA& ADAM VANCUSKI FAMILY

NAME	BORN	DIED	SPOUSE	BORN	DIED	MARRIAGE etc.
1. Paulina Vancuska	June 4, 1859 Parchowo	Sept 13, 1939	Adam Vancuski		Feb 27, 1921	Feb. 8, 1875 in Brudnell
Children:						
1. Augustina Blascavitch	Feb. 11 yr. unknown	June 17, 1949	John Blascavitch Stephen Dota	Dec	Dec. 1941	
2. Martha Dota			Martin Dota			
3. Annie Lawlor	Feb. 16, 1880	Dec. 13, 1980	Phillip Lawlor		Dec. 18, 1942	
4. Mary Gazell			Jack Gazell			
5. Felix Vancuski		1965	Paulina Matcheski		1925	
6. Ethel Hooper			Charles Hooper			
7. Tessie Freeman			Fred Freeman			
8. Stephen Vancuski						He never married
9. Pauline Bassett			John Bassett			
10. Barbara Vancuska	1897	1907				Died of diphtheria at age 10.
11. John Vancuski		1940				Died in the mines.
12. Joseph Vancuski		1907				Died of diphtheria.
13. Agnes Picotte	Mar. 16, 1904	Apr. 3, 2003	Lawrence Picotte	Sept. 19, 1902		

Family Tree of *PAULINA VANCUSKA*

Augustina Blaskavitch (Vancuska)
1st Marriage

NAME	DIED	SPOUSE	DIED	MARRIAGE etc.
I. Lucy Prince	May 28, 1928	John Prince	Jan. 10 1981	
Children:				
1. Adolph Prince		Jean		*Also known as Eddie, Lived in England, served in WWII and married a war bride
2. Mary Rumleskie	1982	Peter Rumleskie		
Ch: Jerome		Louise		* Jerome died tragically and is presumed buried in Galt, ON where his wife continues to live
Lorenzo				
Jacqueline		1? Gilmour		
		2. Norm Laybourne		
Othelia		? Brown		
Angela				*Angela is married but surname is unknown.
3. Frank Prince	1920- 1990	Hertha Kuno		
Ch: Shirley Verch		Delmar Verch		
a. Larry				
b. Wade				
Joan Welk		David Welk		
a. Brian				
Allen Prince		Mary Connor		
a. Todd				
b. Amy				
Roger Prince		Heather Soikie		
a. Tanya				
b. Erin				
Nancy Prince				
Patsy Prince				
a. Chad				
Wendy Markus		Leonard Markus		
a. Josh				
4. Celestine Dombroskie	1921-1990	Dominic Dombroskie	1911-1985	Aug. 15, 1939
Ch: Catherine Andress	1975	Peter Andress		
a. Scott				
b. Michael				
c. Terry				
d. Debbie				
e. Diane				
f. Linda				

Bernice Recoskie		Donald Recoskie		Oct. 14, 1961
a. Donald Jr.		Ann Robertson		
b. Ronald		Nancy Irving		Oct. 3, 1987
i. Sarah				
ii. David				
c. Mary Hirsch		Steven Hirsch		Feb. 21, 1997
i. Sydney				
d. Jane				
Agnes Sernoskie		Leonard Sernoskie		Feb. 27, 1965
a. Sandra				
b. Michael				
c. Brenda				
d. Barry	Mar. 29, 1990			
Terrance Dombroskie		Grace Wagner		
5. Lucy Couroux		Jerry Couroux		
6. Florence Cotie		Joseph Cotie		* Florence and her husband had 13 children and lived in Deep River at the time of her death.
7. Eleanor Auger		? Auger		* Oct. 2003 her husband passed away and she continues to live in Burlington, ON.
II. Rosie Soikie		Herb Soikie		
Children:				
1. Anne Charles		Bob Charles		
Ch: Arnold				
Sidney				
Stanley				
Carl				
2. Joseph Soikie		Myrtle Antler		
Ch: Eldon				
Heather		Roger Prince		
a. Tanya				
b. Erin				
Basil				
Douglas				
3. Genevieve Chapeskie		John Chapeskie		
Ch: Marie				
Joan				
Bernice				
Darlene				
4. Rudolph Soikie		Dolores Burke		
Ch: Larry				
Heather				
Andrew				

5. Harold Soikie		Georgette St. Louis		
6. Theresa Myles		Edward Myles		
Ch: Doris				
Brenda				
Sharon				
Gail				
Danny				
David				
Kim				
7. Arthur Soikie				Died as an infant
8. Paul Soikie				Died as an infant
9. Marcella Mask	Mar. 17, 1999	1. Vincent Pecoski		
		2. Paul P. Mask	May 11,1988	
Ch: Elizabeth		C.J. Grear		
a. Lucinda				
b. Lacey				
c. Jeff				
Clair-Ann		David Chartrand		
a. Jeffery				
b. Greg				
c. Lisa				
Rebecca		Jeff Warren		
a. Candice				
b. Courtney				
10. Thomas Soikie		Joan Hildebrandt		
Ch: Corrina				
Katrina				
Anita				
Colleen				
11. Clarence Soikie		Evelyn Woito		
Ch: Alfred				
Curtis				
Randy				
Sheila				
12. Mary Soikie				Died as an infant
13. Rose Marie Chapeskie		Gerald Chapeskie		
Ch: Melvin				
Gail				
14. Anthony Soikie		Isabel ?		
Ch: Patrick				
Glen				
III. Victoria Steffan	1900-1960	Martin Steffan		
Children:				
1. Ambrose Steffan				
2. Dorothy Steffan				
3. Therista Steffan				
4. Robert Steffan				
5. Bernard Steffan				

6. Esther Steffan 7. Mary Steffan 8. Agnes Steffan 9. Basil Steffan 10. Jimmy Steffan 11. Cecille Steffan				

IV. Theodore Blascavitch
Children:
    1. Anthony Blascavitch
 	
    Ch: Louise
       Sylvain
       Benoit
       KathleenMaheux
       Natalie Maheux
    2. Peter Blascavitch
    Ch: Carol
       Gary
       Nancy
    3. Catherine Prince
 	
    1st Mar: Richard
       Mildred
    2nd Mar: Joanne
       Lori
    4. Arthur Blascavitch
    Ch: Catherine
       Michael
       Francis
       Timothy
       Sharon
       Joanne
    5. Theresa Lukasavitch
    Ch: Glen
       Maria
       Francis
       Rose Anne
    6. Clare Smaglinskie
    Ch: John
       Daniel
       Darcy
       David
   7 Clarence Blascavitch
    Ch: Deborah
       Bradley
		Annie Recoskie
		
		1. Monique Dupuis
		2. Simone Maheux
		
		Anastasia Kosnaskie
		
		1. Anthony Lukasavitch
		2. Bernard Prince
		
		Wilhomene Houwen
		
		John Luckasavitch
		
		Zigmond Smaglinskie
		
		Delores Smaglinskie		

V. Annie Buch
Children:
    1. Ambrose Buch
    Ch: Christopher
       a. Kyle
       Rhonda
	1906- 1967	Frank Buch
		
		Janet Tomchick
		Donna ?
		
		Dan Walker
			1902-1962	

Nancy		1. Robert Warren		
2. Rose Lewyllen		2. Richard Lewyllen	1986	
3. Barbara Visneskie		1. Brian Bleskie		
		2. Tommy Visneskie		
Ch: Jennifer		Jack Whitley		
a. Jessica				
b. Jenna				
Maureen		Tony Gillroy		
Glen Bleskie				
4. Leonard Buch		Marcella Yantha		
Ch: Danny		Mary Jane Rienes		
Ralph		Diane St. Louis		
Janice		Scott Watkin		
Sharon		Walter Schajnoka		
5. Agnes Haugen		Norm Haugen		
Ch: Patricia				
Kevin				
Paula				
Jeffery				
Jackeline				
6. John Buch				
7. Margaret Jackson		Albert Jackson		
Ch: Elizabeth		Stephen ?		
Valerie				
Adrienne		Marc Barrett		
8. Florien Buch		Sheila Enright		
Ch: Kimberly		Perry Crozier		
Stephen		Sonja Warren		
Glen				
Michael				Died at 7 years of age.
9. Sylvester Buch	Jan. 1945-1953			
10. Louie Buch		Brenda Knuth		
Ch: Pamela				
Melissa				
11. Albinus Buch		Colleen Ruddy		
Ch: Anna				
VI. Mary Roberts	Jan. 31, 1908-1990	William Roberts	Deceased	*There were six grandchildren. Spouses unknown.
Children:				
1. Bill Roberts				
2. James Roberts				
3. Kenneth Roberts				
4. Donald Roberts	Deceased			

Augustina Dota (Vancuska)
2nd Marriage

NAME	DIED	SPOUSE	DIED	MARRIAGE etc.
VII. Martha Dota				Died as an infant.
VIII. Clara Coulas		Lawrence Coulas	June 10, 1984	No Children
IX. Agnes Hawkins Children: 1. Paul Leheay 2. Glen Leheay 3. Wayne Leheay		1. Ernest Leheay 2. Garnet Hawkins		

Martha Dota (Vancuska)

NAME	DIED	SPOUSE	DIED	MARRIAGE etc.
I. Robert Dota	Deceased	Elenor Maika		
II. Mary Dota				

Annie Lawlor (Vancuska)

NAME	DIED	SPOUSE	DIED	MARRIAGE etc.
I. Evelyn Hern				Spouse's names and children are unknown.
II. Lawrence Lawlor				
III. William Lawlor				

Marie Gazell (Vancuska)

NAME	DIED	SPOUSE	DIED	MARRIAGE etc.
I. Frances Brown		Name unknown		

Felix Vancuski

NAME	DIED	SPOUSE	DIED	MARRIAGE etc.
I. Alice Vancuskie				Died in infancy, twin of Florence.
II. Florence Vancuskie				Twin of Alice, never married
III. Mary Monica Kubisheskie Children: 1. Ronnie Kubisheskie 2. Carolyn Belanger 3. Susan Elie 4. Irene Cashubec 5. Marlene Mask 6. Andrew Kubisheskie	Aug. 2/03	Felix Kubisheskie Rose ? Paul Belanger Richard Elie Kevin Cashubec Gary Mask Marlene Cybulski	May 2, 1982	June 11, 1946

Ch: Zachary
    Dylan
    Drew
7. Patricia Yantha
8. Timmy Kubisheskie
9. Doreen Price
		Frank Yantha
		
		Lowrie Price		

IV. Evelyn Cybulski Children: 1. Janice Garett 2. Greg 3. Debbie 4. Wayne	 1978	1. Benedict Blank 2. Bronas Cybulski Barry Garett		
V. Dorothy Kovacs Children: 1. Karen Smith 2. Wade Kovacs 3. Will Kovacs 4. Brian Kovacs	Apr. 18, 19??	Bill Kovacs		They had 8 grandchildren. Names of spouses and grandchildren are unknown.

Ethel Hooper (Vancuska)

She married Charles Hooper and children and grandchildren are unknown.

Tessie Freeman (Vancuska)

She married Fred Freeman and children and grandchildren are unknown.

Stephen Vancuski

He never married.

Pauline Bassett (Vancuska)

NAME	DIED	SPOUSE	DIED	MARRIAGE etc.
I. Elaine Bowes		Edward Bowes		Children and grandchildren unknown.

Barbara Vancuska

She was born in 1897 and died of diphtheria at age 10 in 1907

John Vancuskie

He died working in the mines in 1940.

Joseph Vancuskie

He died in 1907 of Diphtheria.

Agnes Picotte (Vancuska)

NAME	DIED	SPOUSE	DIED	MARRIAGE etc.

I. Elaine Gregoire
 	
Children:
    1. David Gregoire
    Ch: Jeremy
    2. Paul Gregoire
    Ch: Jody
        Pamela
    3. Nancy Bunce
    Ch: Mathew
    4. Michael Gregoire
	Nov. 23, 2000	Parnell Gregoire
		
		Brenda Foss
		
		Linda O'Brien
		
		Phillip Bunce
		
		Julie ?
				Nov. 9, 1953

II. Robert Picotte
Children:
    1. Kathy Findlay
    Ch: Tania
        a. Cassidy
    2. Joe Picotte
    Ch: Lindsay
    3. Steve Picotte
    Ch: Samantha
        Anthony
	Mar. 7, 2003	Bernice Rabishaw
		
		Gary Findlay
		Sean Dashnay
		
		Sherry Hartland
		
		Dawn Burly
				1954
				
				Grandchild Madison

Mr. and Mrs. Martin Steffan shown celebrating their 60th wedding anniversary.
Collection of Barry's Bay This Week

Elaine and husband Parnell Gregoire (nee Picotte) and their family taken in 1996.
Collection of Rita Maher

Elaine and husband Parnell Gregoire (nee Picotte) taken at a friend's party in 1994.
Collection of Rita Maher

Excerpts taken from Barry's Bay This Week: Annie Lawlor, a daughter of Adam and Paulina Vancuskie (nee Biernacki) a native of Barry's Bay celebrated her 100th birthday on February 16, 1980 in Fort Frances, Ontario. She was born in 1880 in Barry's Bay and married to Phil Lawlor who was a station agent in Barry's Bay. After leaving Barry's Bay, they moved to Pinewood where her husband was a station agent there for 35 year. When her husband died in 1942, she moved to Fort Frances to be close to her son Bud and his family.

Left to right- Dorothy Kovacs, Ethel Hooper, Monica Kubesheskie, Evelyn Cybulski (all nieces) and Nora Lawlor (daughter- in law) and Annie Lawlor (sitting). *Collection of Barry's Bay This Week*

THE FAMILY

OF

JOHN & AUGUSTINA NEE (RETZA)

BIERNACKI

Family Tree of JOHN & AUGUSTINA (RETZA) BIERNACKI

NAME	BORN	DIED	SPOUSE	BORN	DIED	MARRIAGE etc.
1. John Biernacki	Oct. 23, 1863	June 13, 1949	Augustina Retza	June 16, 1872		Nov. 4, 1890 Wilno
Children:						
1. Joseph Biernacki	April 8, 1895	Nov. 19, 1986	Annie Steffan	April 17, 1905	1986	Nov. 24, 1925
2. Barbara Kulas	1896	1963	Phillip Kulas			
3. Annie Finnerty			John Finnerty			

Family Tree of JOHN BIERNACKI

Joseph Biernacki

NAME	DIED	SPOUSE	DIED	MARRIAGE etc.
I. Raymond Biernaski		Frances Stoppa		
Children:				
1. Phyllis Curran		Bill Curran		
Ch: Sean		Samantha ?		
Dawn				
2. Phillip Biernaski		Catherine Chapeskie		
Ch: Catherine				
Joseph				
Emma				
Jed				
3. William Biernaski		Bonnita Sullivan		
Ch: Rylie				
4. Paul Biernaski		Karen Dorman		
Ch: Nicole				
Kyle				
5. Robert Biernaski				
Ch: Brennan				
Ally				
6. Patricia Shalla				
Ch: M.J.				
Jennifer				
Terrie				
7. Yvonne				
8. Tracy Cosentinno		Joe Cosentinno		
Ch: Francessca				
9. Kim				
10. Annita				
Ch: Heather				
Liam				
Peter				
II. Isaiah Biernaskie		Tessie Luckovitch		
Children:				
1. Irene				
2. Joyce				
3. Marilyn				
4. Garry Biernaskie				
5. Kevin Biernaskie		Michelle Rozek		
III. Agnes Herron		1. Phillip Kubesheskie		
		2. Phillip Herron		
Children:				
1. Clarence Kubesheskie				
Ch: Christina				
Derek				
Mathew				

2. Brian Herron
   Ch: Corine
      Kimberly
      Stephen
3. Brenda Stamplecoskie
   Ch: Melissa
      Jesse
4. Barry Herron
5. Bernitta Herron
	Deceased	Linda Yakabuskie
		
		Paul Stamplecoskie
				Died at age 6

IV. Benedict Biernaskie	Nov. 3, 1931- Nov. 3, 1979			Never married
V. Desmond Biernaskie	Jan. 5, 2002			Never married

VI. Elmer Biernaskie
Children:
   1. Sharon
   2. Christine
   3. Lorraine
   4. Darrin Biernaskie
		Nora Plebon	Oct. 6, 1983	

VII. Florence Peplinski
Children:
  1 Rose- Marie Ivenkovic
     Ch: Christopher
       Debbie
   2. Jeanette Chartrand
     Ch: Gregory
   3. Eileen Warlow
     Ch: Kerry Ann
       Laura
       Daniel
   4. Emmett Peplinski
    Ch: Jill
       Ashby
   5. Audrey Reimer
    Ch: Jenna
       Derek
   6. Linda Norlock
    Ch: Julie
   7. Ivan Peplinski
    Ch: Jordan Lyn
       Justin
       Travis
		Charlie Peplinski
		
		Bob Ivenkovic
		
		Joe Chartrand
		
		Pat Warlow
		
		Pamela Bower
		
		Rudy Reimer
		
		Danny Norlock		

VIII. Beatrice Yakabuski
Children:
   1. Richard Yakabuski
    Ch: Dylan
   2. Sheila Yakabuski
		Benny Yakabuski	Deceased	

3. Jeffery Yakabuski
Ch: Kimberly
4. Collette
5. Tracy Stamplecoskie
Ch: Lindsay
    Kelsey
6. Laurie Yantha
Ch: Derek
    Natasha
    Shannon
		Lauri Ann Dombroski
		
		Richard Stamplecoski		

IX. Joseph Biernaski
Children:
    1. Debbie
    Ch: Kara
    2. Kelly
    Ch: Jenna
		Joyce Giesler		

X. Ernest Biernaski
Children:
    1. Randy Biernaski
    2. Wendy Lehman
		Carol Ann Yakabuski
		
		Nicole Yaskolski
		Shean Lehman		

XI. Ronald Biernaski
Children:
    1. Kelly Biernaski
    2. Melinda Biernaski
    3. Jeannie Biernaski
    4. James Biernaski
    5. Peggy Biernaski
				Twin of Donald.

XII. Donald Biernaski
Children:
    1. Cindy Howard
    2. Tammy Biernaski
    3. Penny Biernaski
    4. Rachel Biernaski
    5. June Biernaski
    6. Rebecca Biernaski
		Anna Mary Yakabuski
		
		Eric Howard
				Twin of Ronald.

XIII. Phillip Biernaski
Children:
    1st Mar: Angela
    2. Jacqueline
    Ch: Brittany
    3. Brian Biernaski
    2nd Mar: Nathan
    5. Luke
    6. Brandon
		2nd Marriage Rose
		Luckovitch		

Barbara, Mrs. Phillip Kulas (nee Biernacka).
Collection of Dolores Flynn

Barbara Kulas (Biernacka)

NAME	DIED	SPOUSE	DIED	MARRIAGE etc.
I. Benedict Coulas Children:	Apr. 19, 1998	Rita Voldock		

1. Ronald Coulas
     Ch: Jeffery
         Jennifer
         Joanne
		Karen Wagnes		

2. Richard Coulas
     3. Bradley Coulas
     Ch: Christopher
	Sept. 6, 1981	Toni Blaine		

II. Kenneth Coulas Children:	1994	Marilyn Purdy		
1. Laurie Coulas		Stephen ?		

Annie Finnerty (Biernacka)

She relocated to Cobalt, Ontario and married John Finnerty. No further records were located on this family.

THE FAMILY

OF

PAUL & MARIANNA NEE

(YAKUBUSKA)

BIERNACKI

Family Tree of PAUL & MARIANNA (YAKABOWSKA) BIERNACKI

NAME	BORN	DIED	SPOUSE	BORN	DIED	MARRIAGE etc.
1. Paul Biernacki	Feb. 7, 1869	May 27, 1942	1. Marianna Yakabowska 2. Marianna Rekowska	Mar. 21, 1875	1901 June 22, 1968	April 30, 1894 January 25, 1902
Children 1st Marriage: 1. Angus Biernacki	July 14, 1899	Feb. 8, 1988	1. Rose Soikie 2. Mary Warner		Feb. 1940 1971	
2. Anastasia Biernacka	1901					Died as a small child
Children 2nd marriage: 3. Agnes Biernacka	1907	June 29, 1923				Died in a house fire at age 16.
4. Theodore Biernacki						Died as a small child.
5. Julia Peplinska	June 6, 1910	Nov. 14, 1985	Adam Peplinski	Nov. 17, 1907	July 16, 1999	Oct. 14, 1930
6. Mary Peplinska	1912	May 2, 1995	Frank Peplinski			

Family Tree of PAUL BIERNACKI (1st Marriage)

Angus Biernacki

NAME	DIED	SPOUSE	DIED	MARRIAGE etc.

I. Bernadette Mielke
Children:
    1. Marilyn Mielke
    2. Gerald Mielke
 	
    Ch: Elvis
        Melissa
    3. Phyllis Mielke
    4. Barry Mielke
    5. Gayle Mielke
	Jan. 1995
	
	Deceased
		1. Elmer Mielke
		2. Bernie McClelland
		
		1. Pauline Cybulski
		2. Unknown		

II. Stanley Biernacki Stepson: 1. Roland	1977	Mildred ?		
III. Mary Biernacki	Aug. 2001			Never married
IV. Sylvester Biernacki				Never married

V. Jack Biernacki
 	
Children:
    1. Anna Maria Drahorat
      Ch: Michael
          Erik
    2. Rhonda Lee Merkley
      Ch: Deanna
         Samantha
    3. Mary Lou Seyeau
      Ch: Joshua
		1. Ruth Wagler
		2. Miriam Dorothea Snyder
		
		Daryle Merkley
		  ? Coleman
		
		Rodney Seyeau		

Anastasia Biernacka

She was born in 1901 and died as a small child and no other information is available.

THE FAMILY

OF

PAUL & MARIANNA NEE

(REKOWSKA)

BIERNACKI

Family Tree of PAUL BIERNACKI (2nd Marriage)

Agnes Biernacka

Agnes was born in 1907 and died on June 29, 1923 in a house fire at the age of 16.

Theodore Biernacki

He died as a small child and no other information is available.

Julia Peplinska (Biernacka)

NAME	DIED	SPOUSE	DIED	MARRIAGE etc.
I. Geraldine Donegan Children: 1. Helen Crowder Ch: Nathan Bradley a. Damian 2. Mary Donegan 3. Kevin Donegan Ch: Jordan Kyle Ethan	Deceased Deceased	Hector Donegan Doug Crowder Trudy ?		
II. Sylvester Peplinski Children: 1. Robert Peplinski 2. James Peplinski 3. Susan Peplinski		Eileen Radtke Darlene Purdy		
III. Nelson Peplinski		Caroline Radtke-Tate		

Mary Peplinska (Biernacka)

NAME	DIED	SPOUSE	DIED	MARRIAGE etc.
I. Leonard Peplinski Children: 1. Michael Peplinski 2. Rose- Marie Peplinski		Irene Burton		
II. Clemence Peplinski		Iverna Latendresse		
III. Kenny Peplinski				
IV. Mary Ann Peplinski Children: 1. Leslie 2. Christopher				
V. Shirley Peplinski				

Adam and Julia Peplinski (nee Biernacka) taken in Sept. 1982.
Collection of Sylvester Peplinski

THE FAMILY

OF

PETER & ANNA

NEE (LUKASZEWITZ)

BIERNACKI

Family Tree of PETER & ANNA (LUKASZEWITZ) BIERNACKI

NAME	BORN	DIED	SPOUSE	BORN	DIED	MARRIAGE etc.
I. Peter Biernacki	Aug. 31, 1872	Nov. 21, 1913	Anna Lukaszewitz (Luckasavitch)		Oct. 22, 1960	
Children:						
1. Mary Mintha	Mar. 7, 1905	Jan. 1, 1986	Dominic Mintha	June 22, 1912	Feb. 28, 1968	May 16, 1939
2. Barbara Kulas	Jan.22, 1907		Dominic P. Kulas	Jan. 22, 1907	Oct. 13, 1970	Oct. 12, 1937
3. John Biernacki	Feb. 2, 1909	Apr. 18, 1990	Frances Maika	Dec. 3, 1911	Dec. 11, 2000	
4. Phillip Biernacki		Aug. 1942	Margaret Evans			He served in WWII and was killed in action.
5. Frank Biernacki		Apr. 28, 1945				He served in WWII and was killed in action.

Family Tree of PETER BIERNACKI

Mary Helen Mintha (Biernacka)

NAME	DIED	SPOUSE	DIED	MARRIAGE etc.

I. Kenneth Mintha
Children:
  1. Geraldine Mintha
  2. Jeffrey Mintha
  Ch: Emily
  3. Jennifer Mintha
		Margaret MacLaurin		

II. Joan Prince
Children:
  1. Alicia Coulas
  2. Glen Prince
		Clemens Prince
		
		Lambert Coulas		

III. Ronnie Mintha
Children:
  1. Paul Mintha
  Ch: Andrew
      Alexandra
      Adam
  2. John Mintha
  3. Julie Mintha
	Oct 26, 1990	Ann Vitkuskie
		
		Christine Tarling
				Born Aug. 5, 1971

IV. Barbara Goulet
Children:
  1. David Goulet
  2. Paul Goulet
  Ch: Lauren
      Jacob
		William Goulet
		
		Tina Solofa
		Linda Beanish		

Barbara Kulas (Biernacka)

NAME	DIED	SPOUSE	DIED	MARRIAGE etc.

I. Marilyn Schipper
Children:
  1. Stephen Schipper
  2. Kristine Schipper
  3. Terry Schipper
  4. Michael Schipper
	Apr. 3, 1970	Richard Schipper
		
		Joanna Pederson
				Born Mar. 27, 1968

II. Roy Kulas Children: 1. Tracy Kulas		Linda Smacmacpel		Linda originated from Austria

III. Phillip Kulas
 	
Children:
  1. Jeffery Kulas
  Ch: Graeme Kulas
		Joan Bozack
		
		Dawn Lefrenier		

NAME		SPOUSE		
2. Karey Ann Helyer Ch: Brayden 3. Christopher Kulas		Maurice Helyer		

John Biernacki

NAME	DIED	SPOUSE	DIED	MARRIAGE etc.
I. Donald Biernaski Children: 1. Lynn Biernaski 2. Karen Muth 3. Laura Biernaski	Apr 17, 1987	Louise Gower Ralph Muth	Deceased	Born Apr. 15, 1965
II. Peter Biernaski	July 15, 1951			Died at age 5.

Phillip Biernacki

Phillip served in the Cameron Highlands in France in World War II and was killed in action.

NAME	DIED	SPOUSE	DIED	MARRIAGE etc.
I. David Biernaski Children: 1. Michael Biernaski Ch: Virginia Connor 2. Kirk Biernaski		Rosslyn Caiger-Watson Melanie Trachsel		
II. Michael Biernaski Children: 1. Jeff Biernaski 2. Jennifer Biernaski 3. Jay Biernaski		Shirley Docking		

Frank Biernacki

Frank served in World War II and was killed while crossing a canal in Holland.

The Life and Times of PHILLIP & FRANK BIERNACKI

Excerpts taken from the Diamond Jubilee, published in This Week in 1986:

Phillip, a son of Peter and Anna Biernacki (nee Luckasavitch), who was born in Whitney and moved to Barry's Bay with his parents in 1914. After a short education in his younger years, he began lumbering at an early age, due to the death of his father while Phillip was still in his childhood. He may well be remembered for his sports activities while in the bay area, as he excelled in baseball.

After the outbreak of World War II, he enlisted with the Cameron Highlanders in June, 1940 and after receiving his training at Landsdowne Park, Three Rivers and ValCartier, he sailed for England in March, 1941 and was given the regimental number C21564. In October of that same year, he married his English war bride, Margaret Evans, and to this union was born two sons. Phillip was killed in action at Brerville La Robert, France on August 11, 1944. He was the first man from Barry's Bay to give his life in the Second World War. On March 3, 1945, his wife Margaret and her sons came to Canada with one of her sons being nineteen months old from Wales, England and settled here.

Phillip's brother Frank enlisted in the Second World War as well and was given the rank of private. The war on the ground took its heavy toll. Frank Biernaski almost made it through the war, when he was killed on April 28, 1945 at 6:00AM, crossing the Emms Canal in Holland. Another local veteran M.P.P. Paul Yakabuski was there as well. He remembered when the Canadians were crossing the canal in boats and that the boat Frank Biernaski was in, suffered a direct hit. The only one to survive the hit was the officer in charge of the boat.

Pte. Frank Biernacki, a brother of Philip Biernacki, was killed on April 28, 1945 while crossing a canal in Holland. A number of area men were in the general vicinity where Pte. Biernacki was killed.

Picture of Frank Biernacki
Collection of Eganville Leader

Anna Biernacka (nee Luckasavitch),
wife of Peter. *Collection of Barbara
Goulet*

Peter Biernacki. *Collection of Barbara Goulet*

Gravesite of Pte. Frank Biernacki who was killed in action on April 28, 1945, the son of Peter and Anna Biernacki (nee Luckasavitch). *Collection of Barbara Goulet*

A letter written from Frank Biernacki to one is his sisters Mary Mintha in1945.
Collection of Barbara Goulet

This is one of the hand written letter and postcards sent to family members in Barry's Bay by Frank Biernacki while serving overseas in World War II.
Collection of Barbara Goulet

The couple standing at the back are Felix Mask and Margaret Casey while at the bottom are Margaret Jane Evans and Phillip Biernacki on their wedding day.
Collection of Barbara Goulet

Some of our men at war in 1941. Left to right - Lance Corporal John Stamplecoski, Private Frank Biernacki and Lance Corporal Leonard 'Red' Sullivan. Photo taken in Europe.

Men at War: (Left to right) Leonard (Red) Sullivan and Frank Biernacki, both of Barry's Bay, with Frank O'Connor, of Campbell's Bay.

The Eganville Leader, November 11, 1987--Page Eight

Newspaper clippings of Frank Biernacki.
Collection of Barry's Bay This Week and Eganville Leader

Pvt. Frank Biernacki (left) with Lance Corporal Leonard Sullivan. Pvt. Biernacki was killed crossing a canal in Holland, on the last day of hostilities in that area.

Newspaper clipping of Frank Biernacki.
Collection of The Eganville Leader

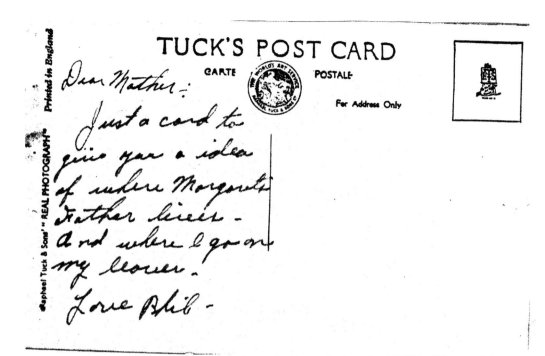

Postcard sent to his mother Anna in Barry's bay by Phillip Biernacki
Collection of Barbara Goulet

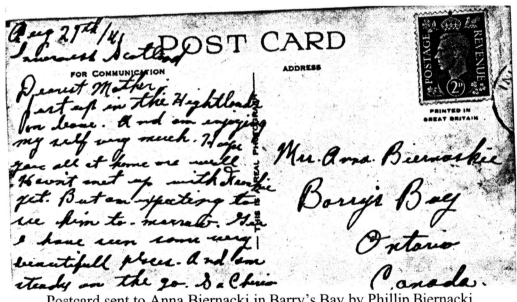

Postcard sent to Anna Biernacki in Barry's Bay by Phillip Biernacki.
Collection of Barbara Goulet

Post Card

Dear Mother

This is the place where I was all summer. But we have since been in 3 other places. And expect to be moving soon again. Also sending a little Xmas Card. Both Marg & I are well

Also some Weather from Scotland

Postcard sent to his mother by Phillip Biernacki.
Collection of Barbara Goulet

Cpl. Philip P. Biernacki, son of Mrs. Anna Biernacki and the late Peter Biernacki, of Barry's Bay was killed in action with the Cameron Highlanders in France. He was the first man from Barry's Bay to give his life in the Second World War.

Picture of Philip Biernacki in uniform while serving overseas.
Collection of Eganville Leader

Lance Corporal Ambrose Burchat (right) with Cpl. Philip Biernacki. The latter was the first man from the Barry's Bay area to die in World War II.

Newspaper clipping.
Collection of the Eganville Leader

THE FAMILY

OF

PHILIP BIERNACKI

Family Tree of PHILLIP BIERNACKI

Phillip Biernacki

Phillip was born in 1876 and left at a young age. No further information is known about him, except a newspaper article that states it was believed that he drowned at Fort Frances on May 25, 1935.

THE FAMILY

OF

STEPHEN BIERNACKI

Family Tree of STEPHEN BIERNACKI

Stephen Biernacki

Information given by Teresa Beanish regarding Stephen Biernacki believed to be born to Antoine and Brigid (Lilla) Biernacki. It was stated he left at a young age and to date no information is available of his birth date or his whereabouts.

After the Pope's passing, I learned that he has had ties to the Barry's Bay and Wilno areas. I felt it was necessary to pay tribute to the life of his holiness, Pope John Paul II in this book.

Karol Wojtyla was born on May 18, 1920, in Wadowice near Krakow, Poland. He is the son of Karol Wojtyla senior; a military officer in the Austro Hungarian Imperial Army, and Emilia Wojtyla (nee) Kaczorowska. Growing up as a young boy, he went to school in Wadowice and lived with his parents in an apartment owned by a Jewish landlord. He was an altar server at St. Mary's Church, across the street from where he and his family lived. He integrated well with his neighbourly Polish and Jewish friends. His mother died on April 29, 1929 of heart failure and he made his first communion two weeks later, at the age of nine years old. One year after his mother died, his older brother Edmund went to study to become a doctor and in December of 1932, he contracted scarlet fever and passed away.

On September 1, 1939, Karol was serving mass, when explosions were heard and he ran home to find his father. They left Krakow because of the Nazi occupation to later return on November 6, 1939. During the occupation many men from the age of seventeen to sixty-five were surrounded and threatened but Karol managed to evade being captured.

During the war, Karol worked in a limestone quarry in very cold temperatures, in which he adapted to working very well under these conditions. The limestone, which they blasted, was taken away by wheelbarrow to a chemical factory. This was a very dangerous job and he witnessed many mishaps. One night he came home late and found his father dead in the apartment that he had shared with him. He prayed and meditated over his body, in which God had inspired him to go on in life. He was an actor, athlete and poet. He also had great interest on pursuing his Polish culture. In 1942, he entered an underground Seminary in Krakow, for fear of the Nazi occupation to study for the priesthood. In 1945, Krakow was liberated and he made final preparations for his priesthood. He was ordained on Nov 1, 1946, and went to Rome to study Philosophy and in 1948, he returned to Poland to be in the charge of a parish.

In 1958, Rev. Father Karol Wojtyla was named Bishop, and was a leader in Poland. After spending forty years of his life in Poland, he returned to Rome in 1962 and in 1967 Bishop Karol Wojtyla was appointed Cardinal by Pope Paul VI. After the death of Pope Paul VI in Aug 1978 it was Pope John Paul I who was elected on Sept 28, 1978 to be Pope and was leader for only 33 days. In October 1978, Cardinal Karol Wojtyla was elected Pope, and he accepted to serve God and his people. He took the name as Pope John Paul II and celebrated his first mass in St. Peter's Square on October 22, 1978. He was the first polish Pope to be elected at the age of fifty-eight since 1523 and the first non-Italian Pope in four hundred and fifty-five years.

On June 2, 1979, he made his first visit to Poland; his native land as a Pope, where millions of people came out to greet him. The Holy Father was charismatic and a very faithful servant of God to a billion Roman Catholics; an extraordinary person not only to Catholics, but other faiths as well. He was an apostle of peace, who defended human dignity and the most recognized Pope of the World as one who believed in Christians, Muslims and Jewish people.

Misfortune took place at St. Peter's Square on May 13, 1981, when the Pontiff was riding through in his entourage. After he had just finished holding a child, he was shot by Mehmet Ali Agca; a Turkish assassin, which sent shock waves throughout the world. The quick response of doctors who performed his surgery, were fortunate to save his life, although it took a long time for the Holy Father to recover. Later Pope John Paul II met with Mehmet Ali Agca in a Rome prison, giving him a blessing and forgiving him for his wrongdoing.

He travelled the world extensively, visiting many countries including making seven visits to the United States and five times when he was Pope. In September 1984, he visited Quebec City, Toronto and Ottawa. His open air masses were attended by thousands of pilgrims.

Excerpts taken from the Eganville Leader quote "Father Stanislaw Kadziolka of Wilno knew Pope John Paul II; at age ten. The priest and Carolus Wojtyla destined to be Pope, attended the same school in Wadowice, Poland, where Carolus had been born."

Rev. Father Mervin Coulas stated "It was when Pope John Paul II was on his Papal visit to Ottawa, that plans were to have the Pope make a brief visit to Wilno, but because of costs and security reasons, the plans were abandoned."

Excerpts taken from the Barry's Bay This Week: "The curvilinear monument, representing the flag of Poland measures six feet by twelve and contains 1, 014 red and white bricks, each brick representing one year of Poland's Christianity, dating back to the year 966. A cast bronze plaque is affixed to the centre of the monument, carrying the following words in Polish and English: The Parishioners of St. Hedwig's honour the First Pope form Poland- John Paul II- dedicating this street in his name- "Karol Wojtyla Street". Three colourful crests adorn the monument: the coat of Arms of John Paul II, bearing the cross with the letter "M" in the honor of Mary, Mother of God, with the Latin inscription TOTUS TUUS (whole yours) exemplifying the Pontiff's total devotion to Mary. Shields of the Kashub Griffin and the Polish Eagle flank the bronze plaque."

Rev. Father Ambrose Pick was parish priest at St. Hedwig's at the time the monument was erected, unveiled and the naming of the street, honouring his holiness Pope John Paul II. It was when the Pope was in Toronto on his Papal visit, that Father Julien Jercha, pastor of St. Anthony's of Padua in Fish Lake, Indiana , a nephew of Msgr. P Biernacki was received by the Pope and was privileged to distribute Holy Communion during the Toronto Papal Mass, as minister of the Holy Eucharist.

Pope John Paul II was firm on issues concerning abortion, euthanasia, woman as priests, same sex marriages, divorces, contraception and for priests to remain celibate. The Pontiff was gifted to speak eight languages and was not afraid to speak his mind and would deeply pray and mediate. On Wednesdays, he made his appearance and gave his blessings to people from the Vatican in St. Peter's Square. He also played a key role in defeating communism in Eastern Europe.

The Pontiff had journeyed to the Northwest Territories, where thick fog prevented the aircraft to make a landing. People gathered there, and were very disappointed, but he assured them to make his visit another time. In 1987, he fulfilled that promise and landed at Fort Simpson, Northwest Territories.

Because of ailing health, Pope John Paul II made his last trip to Canada in 2002, where he went to Toronto to celebrate World Youth Day. There were some 800,000 people who received his spiritual blessing and touched the hearts of so many young people

Holy Week and Easter of 2005 were celebrated and news came of his Holiness Pope John Paul II, our supreme spiritual leader of the Roman Catholic Church that his health was beginning to deteriorate. On Thursday, the last rites or Sacrament of the Sick were administered. His wish was to die at home in his Vatican apartment. On April 2, 2005 at 2:37pm ET at the age of 84 he peacefully passed away. The body lay in state in the Clementina Hall in the Vatican and then St. Peter's Square for public viewing to millions of mourners. The funeral mass was celebrated at St. Peter's Square before mourners on Friday, April 8, 2005. He was interred in the crypt beneath St. Peter's Basilica.

His Holiness Pope John Paul II was a spiritual leader of the Roman Catholic Church for over twenty-six years. He was an apostle of peace, love and devotion from human conception until death and to every man, woman and child of every race in the world, who loved him dearly. Pope John Paul II was the first Polish Pope in history to visit Canada, only leaving his footprints on this globe and will be forever remembered for centuries to come.

Pope John Paul II in prayer
Collection of Marian Helpers

Polish Eagle
Collection of Margaret Biernaskie

Karol Wojtyla Street named after Pope John Paul II in Barry's Bay, Ontario
Collection of Margaret Biernaskie

Monument dedicated to Pope John Paul II Barry's Bay, Ontario
Collection of Margaret Biernaskie

About The Author

Margaret Biernaskie (nee Dombroski) was born on a farm in the hills of Halfway, Ontario now Kaszuby, a daughter of the late Stanley Dombroskie and his wife Jean (Cybulski). At the age of six, the family moved to a farm in Bonnechere, Ontario. She received her education there while growing up, and later obtained employment in Pembroke for four years. In 1965, she joined her future husband Zigmund and departed for Toronto, where she worked for various production companies. In the early 1970's, she and her husband along with son Barry moved to Pembroke, and while raising a family her spare time involved putting her talents to work in carpentry, gardening, etc. It was in Toronto, where she took courses in tailoring and dress designing. In Pembroke she took courses in cake decorating, and for the past 25years she has been specializing in wedding cake design. Aside to sewing, she preferred her saw and hammer. She also began and continues to research family histories of both the Dombroskie and Biernaski generations with her sister Barbara Dombroskie. With future generations quickly growing up, we must preserve our past, so that we can reflect on our grassroots. By publishing this book, she hopes to uncover and piece together the Biernacki Genealogy. Margaret resides in Bonnechere, Ontario with her husband.